Congregational Churches in the United States

Ecclesiastical polity : the government and communion practised by the Congregational Churches in the United States of America : which were represented by elders and messengers in a national council at Boston, A.D. 1865

Congregational Churches in the United States

Ecclesiastical polity : the government and communion practised by the Congregational Churches in the United States of America : which were represented by elders and messengers in a national council at Boston, A.D. 1865

ISBN/EAN: 9783337184810

Printed in Europe, USA, Canada, Australia, Japan

Cover: Foto ©Lupo / pixelio.de

More available books at **www.hansebooks.com**

ECCLESIASTICAL POLITY.

THE

Government and Communion

PRACTISED BY THE

CONGREGATIONAL CHURCHES

IN THE

UNITED STATES OF AMERICA,

Which were Represented by Elders and Messengers in a National Council at Boston, A. D. 1865.

BOSTON:

CONGREGATIONAL PUBLISHING SOCIETY.

1872.

Stereotyped and Printed by
ALFRED MUDGE & SON, BOSTON.

PREFACE.

In the preliminary arrangements for the National Council of Congregational churches which was assembled at Boston, A. D. 1865, three pastors of churches, one each in Connecticut, Massachusetts, and Ohio, were appointed to prepare a paper on "the expediency of issuing a Statement of Congregational Polity." One of the three was unable to participate in the work, but his colleagues presented to the Council their report on the subject assigned to them, and with it a form or draught of a statement of polity for the consideration of the assembled elders and messengers.

The statement thus prepared and submitted was carefully considered; and, having been approved in general terms, was left at the disposal of a large committee, with various suggestions of changes and additions tending to make it more complete, and with authority to publish it after such amendments as they should approve.

The Committee appointed by the Council was so numerous, and so widely dispersed, that any full meeting for consultation was impracticable. But, after ample time for consideration and for advice from all sources, the publication being called for in various quarters, letters were addressed to the members of the Committee, appointing a time and place for their meeting, and requesting every one who could not attend in person, to communicate his views in a written reply. Thus, a careful revision of the proposed Boston Platform of 1865, was effected in the closest practicable conformity with the instructions of the Council; and the revised and amended statement of Congregational polity is now presented to the churches by the surviving members of the Committee.

The usefulness of that Council, great and various as it has been, would have been incomplete without some testimony from it concerning the principles of church government, and the usages in which those principles are applied. Congregational synods in former times have judged it necessary for them to give such testimony. The synod which assembled at Cambridge in 1646, and was continued by successive adjournments till 1648, and to which all the churches of the New-England colonies were invited, left, as a memorial of itself, that statement of Congregational polity which has ever since been called the Cambridge Platform. The synod of Congregational churches which was convened under the patronage of the English government in 1658, at the Savoy in London, issued a " Declaration of the Faith and Order Owned and Practiced in the Congregational Churches of England." Fifty years

later, a synod of the churches in the colony of Connecticut, at Saybrook, gave out that scheme of a modified
Congregationalism, which, though never adopted else-
where, has had its influence on the churches in almost
all parts of our country. More recently, in 1833, the
Congregational Union of England and Wales, though
not properly a synod or council of churches, issued a
careful and well-authenticated Declaration describing
the faith and order of the Congregational churches in
that country. Such precedents were enough to justify
the giving of a similar testimony by an assembly of
elders and messengers representing, for the first time
since 1648, all the Congregational churches in a country which was then an almost unbroken wilderness,
but has now become the United States of America.

Some such declaration, exhibiting with more authority than can belong to any individual or local testimony, the system of order actually held by these
churches. is greatly needed. The churches need it for
their own information and guidance. Pastors and
home missionaries, and, indeed, all our ministers need
it, that they may not be misled by unconscious imita-
tion of systems incongruous with the first principles
of the New-Testament polity. Our foreign missionaries need it, that the churches which they gather may
learn to stand fast in the liberty with which Christ has
made them free. Young men who are preparing themselves in theological schools, for the service of the
churches, need it, that they may be qualified for that
part of their expected work which relates to the rights

and functions of a church, and the administration of its discipline. Many whose ecclesiastical connection is with other portions of Christ's universal church need it, that their minds may be clear of misinformation or of prejudice. Especially is it needed in the new States and territories where ecclesiastical institutions are yet to be formed, and in those older States where all things are becoming new. Wherever devout and believing souls, weary of hierarchical and synodical governments over Christ's free people, are ready to unite in a church which shall be only Christ's, and in which they may joyfully learn and testify that where the Spirit of the Lord is there is liberty, some convenient manual is needed to show them how such a church may be constituted and governed.

No ancient document can be wisely referred to as being in all respects sufficient for the present need of these churches. The Cambridge Platform, though framed with much deliberation and much study of the Scriptures, was the work of a few men, who, in a wilderness remote from all the Christian world beside, were attempting to recover the church polity of the apostles; and it is now more valuable as a means of showing how little our churches have departed from their original principles and methods, than as a guide to the manner in which those principles are now applied and administered in the practice of these churches. Indeed, there are portions of it which, to readers not remembering its date and what questions of church polity were then under discussion in England, or not familiar with the technical terms of a logic now obsolete, are hardly intelligible without a commentary. The Savoy Declaration, though more lucid than the Cambridge Platform, is less systematic; and, as it only touches, instead of exhibiting and applying the great principle of the communion of churches with each other, it is by no means an adequate representation of American Congregationalism. The Heads of Agreement, assented to by certain ministers of Dissenting churches in and about London in 1690, and incorporated into the Saybrook Platform, though it has been useful in Connecticut, and has had its influence in the ecclesiastical history of our country, can hardly be called a statement of Congregational polity. It was designed to mark out a way in which Presbyterian congregations and ministers, actually, though unwillingly, independent of a national church and of Presbyterial judicatures, might walk in amity and virtual unity with Congregational ministers and churches. No statement of polity that was framed in a former century or in another country can suffice for the Congregational churches of the United States, in their present relations to each other, to their country, and to the progress of the kingdom of Christ.

A polemic defence of Congregationalism, or a rhetorical commendation of it, is not what was intended in the original draught of the platform now submitted to the churches, nor what was approved and authorized by the National Council at Boston. Such expositions of our church polity may proceed more fitly from individuals than from any representative body. On the other hand, a simple statement of the two or three first principles which constitute the radical difference between Congregationalism and other theories of church government would not be sufficient. Those first principles are only the points of divergence between differing systems; and how wide the divergence is cannot be shown but by showing the application of the principles. A simple and perspicuous statement, not only of the principles on which our polity is founded, but also of the usages and arrangements which those principles have established among us, and in which, by common consent, they are applied and made practical, will be, it is believed, of great use to our churches both in their internal administration and in their fellowship with each other. Such a statement is what has been attempted in the summary now offered to the churches for their approval, and to all who desire to become acquainted with the ecclesiastical principles and methods of the Congregational churches in the United States.

The authority pertaining to any exposition of Congregational polity, by whatever assembly, is wholly unlike the authority which is claimed for the canons enacted by the variously named assemblies of clergy and delegates which assume to govern the particular congregations under them. It is little more than a truism to say, that the National Council at Boston had no legislative power to ordain a new constitution for the churches, or to promulgate any new rules; and no judicial power to establish precedents which inferior courts must follow. All that any such Council can do is to inquire, to deliberate, and to testify. A careful statement, first approved in general terms by that great multitude of witnesses, and then revised and completed under their directions, by men selected for the purpose from all parts of the country, will naturally have whatever authority belongs to the testimony of trustworthy witnesses, well informed concerning the matter in question, and representing "all those Congregational churches in the United States of America which are in recognized fellowship and co-operation through the General Associations, Conferences and Conventions in the several States." Whatever authority the Cambridge Platform has as testifying what was the way of the New-England churches in 1648, just that authority a similar statement proceeding from the National Council of 1865 may have as testifying what American Congregationalism is in these latter years of the nineteenth century.

Some of us whose names are subscribed, were the compilers of the following statement in the form in which it was presented to the Council. The others were appointed by the Council to aid in revising and completing the statement, so that it might have in its present form the highest practicable authentication from that great assembly. As in the original draught, so in this revision, we have not presumed to insert any novelties, nor to express our own preferences, but only to state what is commonly received and practised in the churches. We dare not profess that we have erred in no particular, nor that in every phrase we are unanimous. Yet while many things of minor importance have been omitted, which some of us desired to affirm, and while every one reserves his liberty of dissent, we have not intended to affirm anything which seemed to any of us unsound in principle or untrue in fact. A comparison of our work with the Cambridge Platform will show how closely we have followed that time-honored summary in the general plan, in the arrangement of topics, and in language; and, at the same time, how freely we have departed from it, whether for the sake of increased perspicuity, or for the sake of exhibiting the Congregational polity as it is in fact to-day, instead of exhibiting it as it was in theory when our fathers, so long ago, were beginning to build on this continent, to the glory of our God, a temple more august than Gothic minster or Roman basilica, — his living temple that shall live forever.

LEONARD BACON,	JULIAN M. STURTEVANT,
ALONZO H. QUINT,	TRUMAN M. POST,
HENRY M. STORRS,	EDWARD BEECHER,
EDWARDS A. PARK,	WILLIAM SALTER,
SAMUEL HARRIS,	JAMES S. HOYT,
SAMUEL C. BARTLETT,	DAVID BURT,
GEORGE P. FISHER,	JOSEPH P. THOMPSON,
JAMES H. FAIRCHILD,	HENRY STOCKBRIDGE,
EDWARD A. LAWRENCE,	NATHANIEL A. HYDE,
JOHN P. GULLIVER,	RICHARD CORDLEY,
BENJAMIN LABAREE,	ASAHEL FINCH,
MARK HOPKINS,	WARREN CURRIER,
WILLIAM BARROWS,	RUFUS ANDERSON.

Hon. WOODBURY DAVIS, of Maine, Hon. JOHN
HALL BROCKWAY, of Connecticut, and Rev. LEONARD
SWAIN, D. D., of Rhode Island, were members of the
Committee for revising and completing the statement
of Congregational polity, but have departed this life.
Yet it should be known that Judge Davis assisted in
the work of the Committee, and that whatever changes
were suggested by him have been adopted.

THE GOVERNMENT AND COMMUNION

OF THE

Congregational Churches in the United States.

PART I.

PRELIMINARY PRINCIPLES.

CHAPTER I.

Definition and Rule of Church Polity.

1. THE Holy Scriptures, and especially the Scriptures of the New Testament, are the only authoritative rule for the constitution and administration of church government; and no other can be imposed on Christians as a condition of membership and communion in the church.

2. God has prescribed in the Scriptures, the association of believers for united worship and spiritual communion, in order to the visibility, the purity, the advancement, and the perpetuity of Christ's kingdom. What God has thus prescribed is the true church polity.*

* Compare Cambridge Platform, ch. 1.

CHAPTER II.

The Church Catholic, and a Particular Church.

1. CHRIST'S Catholic or Universal Church, is the great company of the redeemed and sanctified in all ages.

2. The Church Universal includes the redeemed in Heaven. They who have entered into the joy of their Lord, are the Church Triumphant. They who are serving Christ on the earth, and contending with the powers that rule the darkness of this world, are the Church Militant.

3. The Militant Church Catholic on earth is not merely that which is discerned by God who searches the hearts, but is visible, as including all who profess to believe in Christ, and do not wholly contradict that profession by ungodliness in their lives, or by rejecting the essential truths of the gospel.

4. The Visible Church Catholic comprehends not only such particular churches as are constituted and governed according to rules and precedents given in the Scriptures, but also all assemblies of believers and worshippers, holding what is essential to the Christian faith; and it is rightfully governed by no pretended vicar of Christ, nor by

any assembly having jurisdiction over particular churches, but only by Christ himself through his word and Spirit.

5. As the notion of a visibly organized and governed Catholic Church has no warrant from the Scriptures ; so the notion of a national church having jurisdiction over the particular churches in a nation is equally unwarranted. Under the gospel, the visibly governed church is not ecumenical, nor national, nor provincial, nor diocesan, but only local or parochial, — a congregation of believers dwelling together in one city, town, or convenient neighborhood.

6. A particular or local church is a definite and organized part of the Visible Church Catholic ; and all particular churches, being the one body of Christ, and having one Lord, one faith, one baptism, one God and Father of all, are bound to maintain and manifest the catholic communion of saints, endeavoring, in their relations one with another, to keep the unity of the Spirit in the bond of peace.*

* Compare Cambridge Platform, ch. ii. Savoy Declaration, §§ 1–6. Heads of Agreement, ch. i. §§ 1, 2,

PART II.

THE CONSTITUTION AND ORDER OF THE LOCAL CHURCH.

CHAPTER I.

How a Particular Church is Constituted.

1. THE visible church consists of those who, visibly belonging to Christ, are separated from the ungodly world and united in a holy fellowship.

2. Those who visibly belong to Christ are, *first*, such as, having attained some knowledge of the principles of religion and being free from gross scandals, do profess their personal repentance and faith, and walk in obedience to the word ; and *secondly*, the children of such, who, being children of the covenant, are in that sense Christ's, and are recognized as holy in the Scriptures.

3. The members of one church ought ordinarily to dwell in such vicinity to each other that they can meet in one place ; and ordinarily, the members of one church ought not to be more in number than can meet in one assembly, and manage their

affairs by one administration. Yet if there be many congregations, distinct from each other, in one town or city, they ought to regard themselves and each other as branches of Christ's one Catholic Church in that place.

4. Those believers who dwell together in one place become a church by their recognition of each other, and their mutual agreement to observe Christ's ordinances in one society. Their covenant with Christ to be his disciples and obedient subjects becomes, by that mutual recognition and agreement, their covenant with each other to be fellow-disciples and helpers of each other's faith in a distinct church.

5. Different degrees of explicitness in the church covenant do not affect the being of the church, or the duties and responsibilities of its members. The essence and meaning of the covenant are retained where the agreement of certain believers to meet constantly in one congregation for worship and edification is expressed only by their practice of thus meeting, and their actual observance of Christian ordinances. However explicit the covenant may be, it can rightfully express nothing more than a mutual agreement to observe all Christ's

2

laws and ordinances as one church of Christ; and however informal the agreement, it can mean nothing less.

6. Every believer having the opportunity should be a member of some particular church, that he may honor Christ by his professed conformity to the order and ordinances of the gospel, and that he may have the benefits of visible union and fellowship with the church, which is the communion of the saints. These benefits are, *first*, a participation in the promise of Christ's special presence with his church; *secondly*, the increased activity and enjoyment in the Christian life by combining the affections and endeavors of believers, and by inciting each other to love and good works; *thirdly*, watchful and fraternal help to keep each other in the way of God's commandments, and to recover by due admonition and censure any that go astray; and, *fourthly*, aid in the Christian nurture and training of their children, that their households may be holy, and their posterity be not cut off from the blessings of the covenant. Should all believers neglect this duty of voluntarily entering into organized Christian fellowship, to which duty they are moved by the impulses of a renewed and holy

mind, Christ would soon have no visibly associated and organized church on earth.*

CHAPTER II.

God's Instituted Worship in the Church.

1. Believers joined to each other and to Christ in a church are builded together for a habitation of God through the Spirit. . The church is therefore spoken of in the Scriptures as the house of God and the temple of his worship.

2. The worship of God in his spiritual temple, the church, includes prayer, the singing of psalms and hymns and spiritual songs, the ministry of the word, the sacraments, and the contribution of gifts and offerings for the service of Christ.

3. Prayers in the church should be grave and earnest, lifting up the thoughts and desires of the assembly to God; being prompted by the Holy Spirit, they should not be limited by any prescribed and inflexible form, but offered freely, according to

* Compare Camb. Pl. chs. iii, iv.   Sav. Dec. §§ 7, 8. Heads of Agr. ch. i, §§ 3–5.

the vicissitudes of need and trial, and of joy or sorrow, in the church or in its households ; they should be offered for all men, for those who are in authority, for the welfare of the civil state, and for the Universal Church of Christ on earth ; and in the matter and manner they should be agreeable to such models as the Scriptures give, and, above all, to that model which Christ himself gave to his disciples, that he might teach them how to pray.

4. - Singing in the church is not for the delight of the sense, as in places of amusement, but for the union of voices and hearts in worship, and for spiritual edification. The Psalms in the Old Testament are sanctioned for this use by Christ and his apostles, and remain in the church forever, to be used in praising God. There is warrant also in the New Testament for the use of hymns and spiritual songs, but not to the exclusion or neglect of the Psalms.

5. The ministry of the word in the church is by the reading of the Scriptures, with such exposition as may aid the hearers in their personal and family searching of the same ; and also by preaching and teaching, that the truths and principles which God has revealed in his law and in the

gospel may be set forth distinctly in their manifestation of the glory and government of God, in their relations to each other, and in all their applications to the duties of men and to the salvation of sinners.

6. The two sacraments of the New Testament, representing and commemorating through all ages the twofold grace of God offered in the gospel, are to be administered in all churches. Baptism, wherein the purifying element of water signifies and represents the inward washing of regeneration and renewing of the Holy Ghost, should be administered in simplicity, with no vain or superstitious ceremonies. In like manner the Lord's Supper, wherein believers partake of his body which was broken for us, and of his blood which was shed for many for the remission of sins, is to be celebrated in simple conformity with the recorded words of the institution.

7. In the place of those prescribed and definite exactions which were part of God's appointed worship before the coming of Christ, are the free gifts of Christ's disciples to his suffering brethren and to his cause and service. The contribution in the church is not a secular thing adverse to spiritual

edification, but is an act of grateful homage to Christ and of communion with his brethren.*

CHAPTER III.

Church Power.

1. Church power, under Christ, resides not in any priesthood or clergy, nor in the officers of the church; but in the church itself, and it is derived through the church, to its officers, from Christ.

2. Church power extends no further than to declare and apply the law given in the Scriptures. No church has any rightful power to make itself other than simply a church of Christ, in which his mind, as made known in the Scriptures, shall be the only rule of faith and practice. As no church may add anything to the sum of Christian doctrine, or take anything therefrom, so no church may add anything to or take anything from those rules of Christian living, and those conditions of Christian fellowship, which the Scriptures prescribe. †

---

*Compare John Robinson's Catechism, Qu. 24–37, 46. New Haven Catechism by John Davenport and William Hooke.

† Comp. Camb. Pl. ch. v. Sav. Dec. §§ 1–7.

CHAPTER IV.

Church Officers.

1.   Officers in a church are necessary to its well-being, and to its functions, though not to its existence.   Therefore, they are appointed by Christ's institution, and are counted among the gifts of his triumphal ascension.

2.   The powers and functions of church officers are not to be confounded with those of the apostles, and other extraordinary ministers of Christ at the beginning of the gospel.   Nor are the officers n a church to be recognized as holding their official power in succession from the apostles, or as having any of that authority over all churches with which the apostles were invested.

3.   Church officers, according to the arrangement which the apostles instituted in every church, are of two sorts,— bishops, or elders, and deacons.

4.   The office of elder or bishop, in the church, is twofold: to labor in word and doctrine, and to rule.   As laboring in word and doctrine, elders are pastors and teachers, for the perfecting of the saints, and for the edifying of the body of Christ ; and, in order to this, they are to preach the word

and to administer the sacraments. As ruling in the church, they are to be, not lords over God's heritage, but servants of all, for Jesus' sake, watching for souls as they that must give account. They are to declare the admission of members approved by the church, to ordain officers chosen by the church, to pronounce the excommunication of offenders rejected by the church, and the restoration of penitents forgiven by the church. They are to preside in the meetings of the church, whether for public worship, or for the transaction of its proper business. They are to be guides and leaders in all matters pertaining to church administration, but they cannot perform any act of church power save with the concurrence of the brotherhood. They are to care for the spiritual health and growth of individual members, and to prevent and heal such offences in life or doctrine as might corrupt the church ; and they are to visit and pray over their brethren in sickness, when sent for, and at such other times as opportunity shall serve.

5. The number of elders or bishops in a particular church is not prescribed, but is to be determined by the church itself, in view of its ability and its need. In the primitive churches, a plural

eldership seems to have been the rule, and not the exception. In our American churches, at the beginning, it was thought needful that every church should have at least three elders, of whom two were to labor in word and doctrine, and the other was to be associated with them in all their work as bishops or overseers of the flock. While no church is rightfully subjected to any presbytery exterior to itself, every church should have its own presbytery. The modern usage, concentrating all the powers and responsibilities of the eldership in one person, is founded on convenience only, and is exceptional rather than normal. Whether, instead of one elder, who, under the title of pastor, performs the whole work of the eldership, there shall be two or three, or more, among whom the work of public preaching and the work of ruling and oversight shall be divided, is a question which every church may determine for itself, without infringing any principle of order.

6. Inasmuch as the duty of contributing for suffering members, for the support and advancement of the church, and for the spread of the gospel, is incumbent on all disciples of Christ according to their ability, and is essential to the communion of saints ; and inasmuch as the Lord's Day is espe-

cially designated as a day for such contributions, the church is provided with officers for that service. Deacons are chosen in every church to help the elders, chiefly by receiving the contributions and whatever gifts are offered to the church ; by keeping the treasury of the church ; and by distributing from it for the relief of the poor, especially of those in communion, for the supply of the Lord's table, and, if needful, for the support of the ministry. As almoners of the church, they are to care for the poor, to know them personally, to inquire into their wants and afflictions, and to be the organ of communication between them and the brotherhood.

7. Other officers than bishops and deacons are not provided for a church by any precept or example in the Scriptures. Yet a church may designate any member or members to some definite work in its behalf, such as the work of a scribe or clerk, or that of a superintendent or teacher in its Sabbath school, or that of a committee for some inquiry. In such appointments, the church institutes no new order of officers, but only distributes among its members certain duties belonging to the brotherhood. *

* Compare Camb. Pl. ch. vi, vii. Sav. Dec. §§ 7, 9. Heads of Agr. ch. i, §§ 6, 7 ; ch. v.

CHAPTER V.

Election and Ordination of Church Officers.

1. ˙THOUGH no man may assume an office in the church but he that is called of God, the call of bishops and deacons is not immediately from Christ, but mediately, through the church in which they are to serve.

2. Those who are to bear office in the church should first be proved, and should be known and well reported of as having not only the needful gifts, but also those graces of character which the Scriptures require as qualifications of bishops and deacons.

3. A church being free, none can obtain any office in or over it, but by its own free election; yet to its officers freely chosen the church will yield such respect and helpfulness as are required by the nature of the work which they are to perform.

4. Officers chosen by the church are also to be ordained by it with prayer and, customarily, with laying on of hands. The ordination of an officer is his solemn introduction into the place to which he has been chosen, and is like the inauguration

of a magistrate whose power in the commonwealth comes not from his inauguration but from his election. The ordination of a pastor or teacher is his induction into the ministry of the word ; and if he be afterward dismissed from his eldership in that church, and be called to a like office in another church, it is not, in the modern usage of our churches, deemed necessary that his installation in his new place be with the laying on of hands. Yet, so much the more do we protest against the superstitious notion that consecration to the ministry by imposition of hands introduces the person into a hierarchical or priestly order.

5. In a church which has elders, the laying on of hands is to be performed by those elders. But if the church be destitute of elders, then elders of other churches, or ministering brethren not in office, or (when such help cannot be had) brethren who have not been set apart to minister in the word, may be deputed by the church to perform this service ; and the laying on of their hands with prayer is a sufficient induction of the chosen elders or bishops, no less than of deacons, into their office.

6. Neither a deacon, nor an elder or bishop is

an officer in any other church than that which has
elected him to his office; nor can he perform official acts in another church otherwise than at the
invitation of that church, and by a power derived
through them from Christ; for as no church has
authority over another, so no church can invest its
officers with authority over other churches. *

7. When a member of one church becomes an
officer in another church, his induction into office
ought not to be without the free concurrence of the
church with which he has been in covenant. His
formal dismissal from the one church, followed by
his formal reception into the other, is the most
orderly procedure. Yet the consent of the one in
a council or otherwise, to his induction into office
by the other, may be regarded as a valid transfer-
ence of his membership. Elders or bishops as
well as deacons are to be ordained in every church,
and not outside of and distinct from the churches.

* Compare Camb. Pl. ch. viii–x.   Sav. Dec. §§ 7, 11, 12.
Heads of Agr. ch. i, § 6; ch. ii, §§ 3–6.

CHAPTER VI.

The Maintenance of Church Officers.

1. THE duty of every church to provide an honorable support according to its ability, for the officers who give their time and strength to its service, is expressly enjoined in the Scriptures. Every member of the church, in his place and in the measure of his ability to contribute, is responsible for this duty.

2. Inasmuch as not only the covenanted members of the church, but all who are taught, may be reasonably expected, and should be encouraged, to bear their part in the expense of building the house of worship and sustaining the ministry of the word, provision is made by law, in most or all of the United States, for the civil incorporation of societies or parishes for the support of public worship. The form in which a society may be incorporated for the legal ownership of ecclesiastical property and the support of public worship, is determined by the laws of the State ; but the church, as a spiritual fellowship, electing and ordaining its own officers, and worshipping God according to the New Testament, holds its charter only from Christ,

and may not surrender its spiritual rights and powers to any civil corporation. Therefore the independence of the church in the choice of its own officers, in all its discipline, and in the conduct of its worship, must be steadfastly guarded. At the same time, wherever a parish or ecclesiastical society exists, its right as a legal corporation, to use and expend, within the limits of its trust, the property which it holds for specific uses, must be recognized. While the church is at liberty to elect whom it will, and as many as it will, to be its officers, it cannot, by its own authority, require the parish to support them. For this reason, in the election and settlement of a pastor or other officer who is to be supported by the parish, the co-operation of the parish becomes necessary. *

3. The institution of an ecclesiastical society in connection with the church is sometimes avoided as unnecessary and dangerous. Sometimes, where the laws of the State permit, the brethren of the church become the legal corporation; or membership in the church is made a condition of membership in the society; or the church itself becomes the legal corporation with the power of holding

* Compare Camb. Pl. ch. xi.

property, and manages by its deacons the secular affairs connected with the support of public worship.

CHAPTER VII.

Admission of Members into the Church, and Dismission of Members from one Church to another.

1. THE things which are requisite in all church members are repentance from sin, and faith in Jesus Christ; and therefore these are the things whereof men are to be examined at their admission into the church, and which then they must profess and hold forth in such sort as may satisfy reasonable charity that the things are there indeed.

2. Those who desire to profess their faith in Christ, and to follow him, may be admitted into the church, though weak in the faith, because weak Christians, if sincere, have the substance of that penitent faith and holiness which is required in church members, and such have most need of the ordinances for their confirmation and growth in grace. Such charity and tenderness are to be used, that the weakest Christian, if sincere, may not be excluded or discouraged.

3. It is not needful that the profession of

repentance and faith should be always in the same form of words ; but it must always be in such words as are satisfactory to the church, and must be accompanied by a professed engagement to walk with the church according to the gospel.

4. Such personal profession is required not only of those who have not been before in any church relation, but also of those who, having been born or baptized and brought up in the church, may be considered as in some sort hereditary members ; for they, too, must credibly show and profess their own repentance towards God, and faith towards our Lord Jesus Christ, before they come to the Lord's table, or are recognized as members in full communion.

5. A church member, removing his residence to another place, does not thereby throw off his responsibility to the church with which he is in covenant. If his removal is permanent, he ought to seek, and, unless he is liable to some just censure (in which case he must be dealt with as an offender), he has a right to receive a letter of dismission and commendation to an Evangelical church in the place of his new residence; or, if there be no such church in that place, to any such church with which he can have communion statedly in

Christian ordinances. But his dismission cannot take effect till he shall be received as a member by the church to which he has been commended.

6. A church is not bound to receive a member merely because of his dismission and commendation from another church; but if it find any just ground of objection to him, it may remit the case to the consideration of the church from which he came, and of which he is still a member.*

CHAPTER VIII.

The Method of Dealing with Offenders.

1. THE censures of the church are appointed for the prevention and removal of offences and the recovering of offenders; for purging out the leaven which may infect the whole lump; for vindicating the honor of Christ and of his church, and the profession of the gospel; and for preventing the displeasure of God that may justly fall upon the church if they suffer his covenant to be profaned by notorious and obstinate offenders.

* Compare Camb. Pl. ch. xii, xiii. Sav. Dec. §§ 17, 20, 28. Heads of Agr. ch. i, §§ 3, 8, 9.

2. Censures in the church are of two sorts,— admonition and excommunication.

3. If an offence be private, one brother trespassing against another, the offender is to acknowledge his repentance of it unto his offended brother, who is then to forgive him. But if the offender neglect or refuse to do this, then (1) the brother offended is to go and admonish him privately, between themselves. If thereupon the offender be brought to repent of his offence, the admonisher hath won his brother. But if the offender hear not his brother, then (2) the offended is to take with him one or two more, that in the mouth of two or three witnesses every word may be established, whether the word of admonition if the offender receive it, or the word of complaint if he refuse. (3) If the offender be not recovered by that second admonition, the offended brother is then to tell the church. If the church find that the complaint is well founded, it admonishes the offender; and then if he hear the church, and penitently confess his fault, he is recovered and gained, and is to be forgiven. But if, after being admonished by the church, he be not yet convinced of his fault, and ready to profess, frankly, his repentance of it, he

remains under the censure of admonition, which of itself excludes or suspends him from the holy fellowship of the Lord's Supper, till either the offence is removed by his penitent confession, or the church, after reasonable forbearance, proceeds to cast him out by excommunication.

4. When the offence is already public and notorious, and is of such a character as to be infamous among men, a more summary proceeding is authorized by the Scriptures. The church, without waiting for an individual complaint, or for the effect of private admonition, may take notice of the notorious fact, and cast out the offender without delay, for the mortifying of his sin and the saving of his soul in the day of the Lord Jesus, as well as for the vindication of the gospel which he has dishonored. Yet no offender may be censured without trial and the opportunity of being heard.

5. In dealing with an offender, great care is to be taken that we be neither too rigorous nor too indulgent. Our proceeding ought to be with a spirit of meekness, considering ourselves lest we also be tempted. Yet, the winning and healing of the offender's soul being the end of these endeavors, we must be earnest and thorough, not healing the wounds of our brethren slightly.

6. While the offender remains excommunicated, the church and all its members are to refrain from all communion with him in spiritual things; yet, while there may be any hope of his recovery, they are to be kindly watchful for signs of repentance in him; not counting him an enemy, but admonishing him as a brother.

7. If the censure be made effectual by the grace of Christ, so that the excommunicated person repents of his sin, and with confession desires to be restored, the church is thereupon to forgive him; and, as the censure was public, he is to be publicly absolved or loosed from the censure, and restored to full communion.

8. It is doubtless of great importance to the welfare of the church, that profane and scandalous persons be not permitted to continue in its fellowship and to partake at the Lord's table; and the church which neglects to deal with such members, and to use the discipline of the Lord's house for their reformation or their exclusion, is greatly to be blamed. Yet such a church is not therefore to be immediately forsaken and renounced by those who would live godly in Christ Jesus. Nor is it reasonable that any individual member of that

church should therefore withdraw himself from the
Lord's table.   In so doing, he wrongs his own soul
by denying to himself the appointed means of
grace, and wrongs the church by adding another
scandal to that which he would rebuke.   Let him
rather endeavor, modestly and seasonably, according to his power and place, that the unworthy may
be duly proceeded against by the church to whom
that duty belongs.*

CHAPTER IX.

*Relation of the Church to Civil Government, and the
Conflict of Laws.*

1.   THE right of the church to assemble for worship, to observe Christ's ordinances, to hold forth
the word of life by public preaching and by private
communication, to receive into its communion
those who give evidence of repentance and faith,
and to admonish offenders or exclude them, is not
a mere concession from the civil power, but is part
of that religious liberty which Christ, by command-
ing his gospel to be preached to every creature,

* Compare Camb. Pl. ch. xiv. Sav. Dec. §§ 18, 19. Heads
of Agr. ch. iii.

challenges for all men, and which no human government can suppress or violate, without incurring the displeasure of God.

2. The law which the church administers in its discipline is not merely the law of the land, nor the law of common use and opinion, but the higher law of God as revealed in the Scriptures ; for that which is highly esteemed among men conformed to this world may be abominable to God and to men enlightened by his word and Spirit. If wickedness go unpunished in the civil state, or be even honored by public opinion, it is not therefore to be tolerated in the church. If the law of the land require of any man, under whatever penalties, that which the law of God forbids him to do, or if it forbid him to do what the law of God requires, it is better to obey God rather than men ; and the church is to require of all its members obedience to the higher law of God. Yet, inasmuch as the Scriptures require of every Christian soul subjection to existing powers in the civil state, whether Christian or anti-Christian, the duty of loyalty to the government, of conscientious obedience to every law which does not positively require what God forbids or forbid what God requires, and of patient

submission to persecution or other injustice when there is no lawful redress, is a duty of religion which the discipline of the church must honor and maintain.

3. With matters exclusively political the church as such has no concern ; for Christ's kingdom is not of this world. But with matters of morality and religion, the church, in the administration of its discipline, and in the testimony which it is to give for God, has much to do. Especially in a free commonwealth, where the government proceeds continually from the people, the church is bound to testify, in its discipline and in its' teaching, against wicked laws and institutions, not fearing to assert and apply the law of God as revealed in the Scriptures, whatever may be the contradiction of sinners, and whatever the conflict between that supreme law of Christ's kingdom and the laws ordained of men, or the institutions and usages of society. Thus the moral sense of communities and nations must be corrected and enlightened, and must be made to advance with the progress of the church, till Christ shall be honored in all lands as King of kings and Lord of lords, the blessed and only Potentate.*

* Compare Camb. Pl. ch. xvii. Heads of Agr. ch. vii.

PART III.

THE COMMUNION OF CHURCHES.

CHAPTER I.

Principles and Specifications.

1. ALTHOUGH churches are distinct, and therefore may not be confounded one with another;
and equal, and therefore have not dominion one
over another; yet all the churches ought to preserve church communion one with another, because
they are all united to Christ as integral parts of
his one Catholic Church, Militant against the evil
that is in the world, and Visible in the profession
of the Christian faith, in the observance of the
Christian sacraments, in the manifestation of the
Christian life, and in the worship of the one God
of our salvation, the Father, and the Son, and the
Holy Ghost.*

2. The communion of churches with each other
is manifested in various acts of fraternal comity,
correspondence, and helpfulness:

* Compare Camb. Pl. ch. xv, § 1.

(1.) In mutual recognition ; one organized congregation of Christian worshippers acknowledging another to be a visible church of Christ, and each professing a readiness to interchange with the other all reasonable acts of Christian courtesy and love.

(2.) In admitting members of one church to commune, as such, at the Lord's table in another church, and refusing to admit them if they are under censure.

(3.) In permitting and inviting a minister of, the word, recognized and accredited as such by one church, to speak for Christ in another church.

(4.) In the dismission and reception of members, when for any sufficient reason, they pass from one church to another.

(5.) In giving and receiving advice when one church desires counsel of another, or of many others.

(6.) In giving and receiving help ; as when one church gives of its members that another may be supplied with officers ; or, as when one church receives outward support from the contributions of another, or of many others.

(7.) In consultation and co-operation for each

other's edification and prosperity, or for the common interest of the gospel.

(8.) In giving and receiving admonition; as when there is found in a church some public offence which it either does not discern, or neglects to remove; for though churches have no more authority one over another than one apostle had over another, yet as one apostle might admonish another, so may one church admonish another, without usurpation; in which case, if the admonished church refuse to hear its neighbor church and to remove the offence, it violates the communion of churches.*

3. The churches of the Congregational polity, as integral portions of Christ's catholic Church, maintain all practicable communion with all other portions of the Church universal. While other churches differ from us in their internal polity, in their relations and connections with each other, in their forms of worship, or in the uninspired statements and definitions of doctrines disputed among Christians, and while we disown their schemes of hierarchical or synodical government, we acknowledge as particular churches of Christ all congregations of Christian worshippers that acknowledge the holy

* Compare Camb. Pl. ch. xv, § 2.

Scriptures as their supreme rule of faith and practice, and Christ as the Lamb of God who taketh away the sin of the world. We pray for their peace and prosperity. We invite their members to occasional communion with us in worship and in sacramental ordinances. We receive their letters of dismissal and commendation, and, in return, dismiss our members, as occasion may require, with letters of commendation to them. We are ready to be edified by their ministers. And, in all reasonable and hopeful methods, we are ready to consult and co-operate with them for the advancement of the gospel.*

4. As some acts of the communion of the churches are due, in one degree and another, to all the integral parts of Christ's catholic Church, so other acts of communion are specially due from churches instituted and governed according to the Congregational polity to other churches instituted and governed according to the same polity. Certain acts of communion are not practicable between churches congregationally governed and churches that are under a hierarchical or synodical government ; and certain acts of com-

* Compare Sav. Dec. § 29.

munion are not practicable between churches which
seriously differ from each other in the systems of
doctrine which they deduce, respectively, from the
Scriptures, even though they recognize each other
as holding that faith which is necessary to salvation. A church desiring the approbation and assistance of other churches in the ordination of its
officers cannot wisely or courteously ask such
approbation and assistance from churches in whose
professed theory of government all ordinations must
be by a prelate, or in whose theory the power of ordination is given only to a presbytery ruling over many
congregations. In like manner, if it desire counsel
in any case involving questions of doctrine, it cannot
wisely or courteously ask such counsel of churches
not accepting that general system of doctrines
which is the well-known basis of mutual confidence and intimate communion among evangelical
churches of the Congregational polity.

5. The more intimate communion existing among
these churches is exercised in asking and giving
counsel, in giving and receiving admonition, in
various acts of helpfulness towards churches need-
ing help from others, and in conferences and consultations for the parochial revival and prosperity

of religion, or the general advancement of Christ's kingdom.*

CHAPTER II.

Councils.

1.   COUNCILS of churches, orderly assembled, to declare the opinion of the churches on any matter of common concern, are important to the communion of the churches.   That scriptural example where the church at Antioch sent messengers to the church at Jerusalem for consultation and advice in a difficult question, is a sufficient warrant for such councils.   In respect to the calling of councils, the manner of their proceeding, and the authority conceded to them, the usage of the churches, guided by the Scriptures, and those principles of equity and wisdom which the Scriptures recognize, has established certain rules tending to order in the despatch of business, to the avoidance of unnecessary strifes, and to the edification of the churches.

2.   The churches invited to assist in a council are represented by messengers or delegates chosen by them for the particular occasion.   By ancient

* Compare Sav. Dec. §§ 25-27.   Heads of Agr. ch. iv, vi.

usage, the pastor of a church, having been duly recognized as its presiding elder or bishop, is always expected to be one of its messengers; and the letters convening the council invite each church to be represented by its pastor and delegate. Yet in the council, when convened, there is no distinction of authority between pastors and other delegates.*

3. It is manifest, from the reason of the case, that in ordinary cases a council ought to be made up chiefly of churches in the near vicinity. But when a council is called to advise in some personal or parochial controversy which involves strong sympathies and interests in the surrounding region, it may be expedient to ask counsel from more distant churches rather than exclusively from those near at hand.

4. A council is to be called only by a church, or by an aggrieved member or members in a church which has unreasonably refused a council, or by a competent number of believers intending to be gathered into a church. In a difficulty or controversy between the church and its elder or elders, or between the church and some other person or

* Compare Camb. Pl. ch. xvi, § 6.

party in the church, if a council is desired, and the church consents, the churches to constitute the council are selected by agreement between the parties, and are invited by letters-missive from the church ; and this is called a mutual council. If a church unreasonably refuses to call a mutual council (the matter of grievance, on which the advice of other churches seems desirable, having been distinctly stated in connection with the request for such a council), then an *ex parte* council may be invited by letters-missive from the aggrieved member or members.

5. An *ex parte* council, properly called, has the same standing, and is entitled to the same respect, as a mutual council ; for it were unreasonable that, in case of grievance, either party should be deprived, by the obstinacy of the other, of such relief as the neighboring churches could give. But that it may be properly convened, it is requisite, (1) that there be proper ground for calling a council ; (2) that one party, properly requested, has unreasonably refused to join in calling a mutual council ; (3) that the *ex parte* council be called, upon the statement of the original grounds for asking a council, and of the unreasonable refusal of the

other party to join ; and, (4) that the churches invited be impartially selected. When assembled,
the *ex parte* council should first offer itself to the
refusing party as a mutual council.

6. Councils, ordinarily and fitly, consist of
churches invited and consenting ; though sometimes individuals whose advice or aid in the council is deemed important are personally invited.
After being called, no church or person can be
added to or taken from the proper members in any
manner. For the letters-missive having specified
the churches and persons invited, and the matters
to be laid before the council, each church appointed
its delegates upon its knowledge of the questions
on which its advice was requested, and of those
churches or individuals with whom it was to be
associated in giving advice. Nor, for the same
reason, can the council act on any matters which
are not distinctly stated in the letters-missive.

7. Councils are not to be convened upon every
ground of dissatisfaction with a church, nor in
cases of light moment. They are proper only
upon some matter of common interest to the
churches ; such as relations of fellowship between
churches, or the relation of a member to the com-

4

munion of other churches ; the relations of pastors and churches ; the reputation of the brotherhood of churches, as affected by the acts or condition of a church ; or matters of general interest to the cause of Christ. They are in no such sense courts of appeal that they may alter or rescind any act of a church. Yet in cases of censure, if the proceedings complained of are found to have been in gross violation of the rules given in the Scriptures, the council may advise and declare that in its judgment the censure complained of is wrong, and may commend the censured person to be received by some other church as a member in full communion.

Particular occasions for councils are such as these :—

(1.) When a competent number of Christian brethren propose to unite in a church covenant, and desire to be recognized as a church in the more intimate communion of the Congregational churches, the ordinary and most orderly method of obtaining such recognition is by an ecclesiastical council, invited for that purpose by their letters to a convenient number of churches, and especially of churches in the near vicinity. Having given to that council, when assembled, a satisfactory state-

ment of their faith and order, and of the reasons
for their becoming a distinct church, together with
sufficient evidence not only of their Christian character, but also of their fitness in respect to gifts
and numbers for performing the duties of a church,
they receive as a church the right hand of fellowship extended to them by the council in behalf of
all the churches.*

(2.) The induction of a pastor or teacher into
his office, in any church, or, on the other hand, the
dismission of such an officer from his place, concerns the communion of the churches. Therefore,
an ecclesiastical council is convened for the ordination or public recognition of a pastor, and, in
like manner, for his dismission at his own request.
A due respect to the communion of the churches
requires that no man assuming to be a pastor of a
church shall be acknowledged as such by other
churches, unless, at or after his entrance on the
duties of the office, he has been publicly recognized
by receiving the right hand of fellowship from
neighboring churches through a council convened
for that purpose. The welfare of the churches, in
their intimate communion with each other, requires

* Compare Camb. Pl. ch. xv, § 3.

this safeguard. In like manner, the communion of churches requires that no minister dismissed from his charge shall be regarded as having sufficient credentials of his good standing unless he is duly commended by a council convened on the occasion of his dismission. *

(3.) When difficulties, whether internal or external, threaten the peace and spiritual prosperity of any church, and are not likely to be adjusted without aid, or when any question arises on which the church needs advice for the guidance and correction, or confirmation, of its own judgment, that church has a right to ask the advice of other churches with which it is in communion. To such an advisory council the trial of a difficult case is sometimes referred. The council, having examined the questions referred to it, whether questions of fact or questions of principle and duty, pronounces its conclusions ; but it has no power to inflict any church censure, or to absolve from censure. It can only advise the church ; and the church, by accepting and adopting the result of the council, carries the advice into effect.

(4.) When a member against whom charges

* Compare Heads of Agr. ch. ii, §§ 4-6

have been preferred, requests the calling of a council for the trial of those charges, and the church
consents to the request, or when, in any manner,
parties have arisen who desire a council for the
hearing of the questions between them, the
churches to constitute the council are mutually
agreed upon between the parties. Yet a mutual
council is not convened in the name of the parties,
but in the name of the church. In such cases, a
refusal on the part of the church to call a council
before trial, or at the request of such parties, does
not give any occasion for an *ex parte* council.

(5.) When a member, having been excommunicated or excluded by the church, conscientiously
protests that the censure or exclusion is not according to the facts, or that it is not warranted by
the word of God, he may respectfully ask the
church to join with him in calling a mutual council
for a new hearing of his case; and, that request
being denied by the church without sufficient
reason, he may appeal to other churches for advice, and for such relief as they may find reason to
give him, and may invite them to meet in an *ex
parte* council. Or when a portion of any church
has been seriously aggrieved by such action or

non-action of the church as causes public scandal to the cause of Christ, and their request for a council has been denied by the church, they may in like manner appeal to other churches for a hearing of their cause and for advice concerning their duty. But it must be remembered that a mere difference in judgment between a church and any minority of its members, on a question of expediency or a matter of doubtful disputation, is neither a grievance to the minority, nor a scandal calling for fraternal admonition or advice from other churches.

(6.) When a member liable to no just censure has requested letters of dismission and recommendation to some other recognized church, and the request is refused, he may request the church to invite a council to hear the case ; and, if the church refuses, he may himself ask a council to give him relief.

(7.) When a pastor or other ordained minister in any church is charged with offences which would render it proper that he be deposed from the ministry, then the church should invite a council to examine the charges ; if they be proven, the council should advise that he be no longer recognized as a Christian minister. The decision of the council in such a case is binding and conclusive. A second council cannot revise it, unless by consent of both parties, the church and the accused; and courts of law will act upon it without inquiry into its correctness.

8. The council, when assembled, organizes itself by the choice of a moderator and scribe, that its proceedings may be orderly and deliberate, and may be duly written down for the use of those whom the result concerns. If a majority of the churches invited be not represented, those present ought not to proceed as a council unless the party inviting consents. Being a representative body, its functions are limited to the subjects specified in the letters-missive. In voting, it was an ancient and laudable custom that each church give its voice as a church, and not that the messengers vote as individuals; but this custom is not universal. Having properly deliberated, and made up its decision, the council is forthwith to be dissolved; and the scribe is to convey a copy of its proceedings and advice to the parties concerned.

9. The decision of a council is, in most cases, only advisory. Yet, even when the parties have

not bound themselves beforehand to be governed by the advice of council, the decision, if not contrary to the Scriptures, is to be reverently accepted as the voice of the churches, and as the reasonable and divinely warranted means of terminating differences that might otherwise work interminable mischief. *

10. When a council, properly convened and orderly proceeding, whether mutual or *ex parte*, has pronounced its advice, a second council upon the substance of the same questions, or upon the advice of the first, is manifestly improper. If both parties desire further light, they may agree thereto. But, if one refuse, an *ex parte* council is in that case not warranted, and is manifestly disorderly.

11. A council orderly assembled to advise concerning the acts and administrations of a church, and finding that such church deliberately receives and maintains doctrines which subvert the foundations of the Christian faith, or that it wilfully tolerates and upholds notorious scandals, or that it persistently disregards and contemns the communion of churches, may, after fit admonition, advise the churches to withhold from that erring church all

* Compare Camb. Pl. ch. xvi, § 5.

acts of communion till it shall give evidence of reformation. Any church, after due admonition, may call a council to advise in such a case.*

12. Some Congregational churches, neighboring to each other, are confederated, more or less strictly, for mutual assistance in cases which require a council. Such confederations, whether under the name of consociation or convention, may be useful if they duly recognize and guard the principle that the power of inflicting church censures and of absolving from censure, and the power of choosing and ordaining officers, and of removing them from office for good cause, reside, under Christ, in the particular church, and not in some ecclesiastical authority extrinsic to the church; and the cognate principle, that councils, however constituted, are for the communion of churches with each other, and not for government over the churches.

CHAPTER III.

CONFERENCES OF CHURCHES.

1. It is fit and convenient for the churches of a neighborhood to meet sometimes, by their pastors and delegates, for the purpose of reporting to

* Compare Camb. Pl. ch. xv, § 2.

each other their spiritual prosperity and progress, and of consulting together how to advance the cause and kingdom of Christ. Such meetings are commonly called Conferences of Churches, and are distinguished from other councils in that they have nothing to do with giving advice to any particular church concerning the ordination or dismission of any of its officers, or concerning the administration of its government. They meet only for mutual information and inquiry, that through them the churches may provoke each other to love and to good works.

2. Conferences of churches are either occasional or stated. Any church may invite neighboring churches, more or fewer, at its own discretion, to meet with it for mutual edification and inquiry. Or a number of churches may associate to hold such conferences at fixed periods and under definite regulations. Stated conferences of the churches have been greatly useful in promoting zeal and Christian activity, and in making the gifts of one church subserve the edification of others.

3. In most of the United States, the several conferences are associated in a General Conference or Association of the churches, which institutes a

careful inquiry every year, and makes its report concerning the general prosperity and progress of the churches throughout the State.

CHAPTER IV.

Synods or National Councils.

1. Occasions may arise in the progress of Christ's kingdom, when a representative assembly of churches, coming together for consultation and agreement and for testimony, is required, which shall be larger in its numbers than any council such as a single church can convene for its own need, and larger in its constituency than any stated conference of churches. Such synods were required, and were held at sundry times, when the fathers of our churches were laying the foundations on which many generations were to build.

2. A synod cannot be constituted by any number of unauthorized individuals assuming to represent the churches. The express consent of the churches, acting severally, in their self-government under Christ, recognizing the call, and sending forth their elders and other messengers, is what constitutes the synod as a representative body.

An assembly thus constituted by the joint action of many churches, and coming together, not for strife and contention, but for devout and earnest consultation concerning things that pertain to the kingdom of God, may be expected to have much of those gracious influences, and of that guidance by the Holy Comforter, in which Christ fulfils his promises: "Lo, I am with you always, even unto the end of the world"; and "Where two or three are gathered together in my name, there am I in the midst of them."

3. The calling of such a synod ought not to proceed from the mere will or motion of unauthorized individuals, nor from the mere motion of any one church acting without consultation. When the elders and other messengers of any considerable body of churches, coming together in a representative assembly, such as the General Conference or General Association of a State, are convinced that an occasion has arisen which requires a national synod or council, they may reasonably institute inquiries by correspondence with other similar bodies; and if, after such correspondence and conference as may conveniently be had, the conviction is strengthened and extended, that, in the

providence of God, there is a call upon the churches to confer with each other in a national council, the arrangements may be made, and the invitation issued by such persons as shall have been desig-nated to that service by common consent in the preliminary consultations. The invitation should be addressed, not to associations or conferences purporting to represent the churches, but distinctly to each several church, so that the ultimate deter-mination of the question shall proceed directly from the churches themselves ; and every church shall have the opportunity of consenting or with-holding its consent according to the wisdom given to it from above.

4. The proper function of a synod is not to legislate for the churches, nor to determine impera-tively any question which is not already deter-mined by the Scriptures, but by inquiry and brotherly conference, with prayer for divine illu-mination, to obtain and hold forth light on such matters as the churches have referred to its delib-erations. A synod, as a great cloud of witnesses, may properly testify in behalf of the constituent churches, not only their common faith in Christ their Saviour, but what is the system of Christian

doctrine, and what the system and theory of ecclesiastical administration, which are the basis of their special communion one with another as churches walking in the order of the New Testament.

[5. In accordance with these principles, the evangelical churches called Congregational (other churches of the same polity being known by other names) have, with general consent, associated themselves under a constitution which provides for the holding of a National Council every third year, beginning with the year of our Lord 1871.] *

CHAPTER V.

Confessions of Faith.

1. NEITHER Christ nor his apostles prescribed any form of words to be imposed on disciples, or on churches, for the confessing of their faith. Had such a form been given, it would have become a part of the canonical Scriptures.

2. Every church is to judge for itself whether the form of words offered or adopted as a confession of faith, by any who desire admission to its

* Compare Camb. Pl. ch. xvi. For the Constitution of the National Council, *see* Appendix.

holy communion, is a satisfactory profession of faith in Christ and his gospel.

3. When a council is assembled for the ordination or recognition of a pastor, or for the ordination of a missionary or other minister at large, the candidate for ordination or recognition may reasonably be required to make a more ample declaration of his religious belief, holding forth to the church and the council, not only his personal faith in the Saviour of sinners, but also his doctrinal soundness as a preacher of the word. Such confession of faith should be in words deliberately and accurately chosen, and the council must judge whether the confession is sound and sufficient.

4. Every church desiring to share in the fellowship of the churches should make some adequate declaration of its fidelity to the doctrine which is according to godliness. It is therefore fit that every church set forth, in the form of a confession or catechism, the system of truth which it receives as the faith once delivered to the saints, which its pastors and teachers maintain by their ministry, and in which it trains its children.

5. Any assembly of elders or messengers representing a body of churches, local or national, is

competent to testify in the form of a confession what system of doctrines is received and maintained in the churches which it represents. Or any body of Christian men, being called thereto in the providence of God, may frame and publish, as a confession of their faith, a declaration of the truths which they receive as revealed from God by his word and Spirit. Such confessions of faith have often been useful for the refutation of injurious reproaches, or for the confirmation of the truth.

6. The right use of confessions of faith is not for separation and mutual exclusion among Christians, but rather for mutual information and confidence, and the manifestation of unity. For this purpose, inasmuch as the Scriptures are often perverted, and doctrines subversive of the faith once delivered to the saints are brought in among the churches, it sometimes becomes reasonable and fit for churches, or for representative assemblies, not only to testify and confess the truth, but also to bear witness against doctrines contrary to the gospel of Christ, and dangerous to the souls of men. For Christian unity is not to be maintained by compromises with doctrines which corrupt the

word of God, but only by adherence to the truth as it is in Jesus. Yet no confession of faith or testimony against error is to be set up in place of the Scriptures, which are the only standard and unerring rule of faith, and with which all human formularies are to be constantly and diligently compared.*

PART IV.

THE MINISTRY.

CHAPTER I.

The Preaching of the Word.

1. WHILE those whom the church chooses and ordains to be its pastors and teachers, are, by virtue of their office, preachers of the gospel, laboring in word and doctrine, the work of preaching is not exclusively a function of church officers. Fit men not bearing office in any church, but giving themselves to the work of preaching, have always been

---

* Compare Preface to Camb. Pl., Heads of Agr. ch. viii. Preface to Savoy Confession.

5

recognized among us as ministers of the word.
The ministry, therefore, includes all who are called
of God to preach the gospel and are set apart to
that work by ordination.*

2. The necessity for a recognized class of ministers not holding office in any church is manifold.
(1.) In preaching the gospel to every creature,
there is much to be done which cannot be done by
elders or bishops of churches, whose work is chiefly
parochial, and not missionary. (2.) There is, and
ever must be, need of ministers, recognized as
such, who can supply, by occasional and temporary
ministration, the lack of service in churches that
have no preaching elders. (3.) Those who are to
teach and train men for the ministry must needs
be ministers, recognized as such among the
churches, and esteemed for their zeal and power
in holding forth the word of life ; and yet they
cannot ordinarily be at the same time officers in
churches. (4.) Under every theory of church
order, there must be, in fact, a class of men accredited in some way, and recognized as qualified by
natural endowments, by learning and study, and
by the work of the Holy Spirit on their souls, to

* Compare Sav. Dec. § 13. Heads of Agr. ch. ii, §§ 3, 7.

preach the word ; among whom the churches may find fit men to be their pastors and teachers. (5.) Nor can the churches consent that when a pastor, for any good reason, resigns his office, and is discharged with commendation as a good and faithful servant of Christ in the gospel, he shall thenceforth cease to be reputed and recognized as a minister of the word. (6.) It is abundantly evident from the Scriptures, that, in the beginning, there were many ministers of the word, beside the elders who were ordained in every church ; and that while the distinctive work of the apostles was essentially extraordinary, ceasing with their lives, and transmitted to no successors, the work of ministers not holding office in the churches was a work which continues and must continue till Christ's Catholic church on earth shall cease to be militant.

3. Such ministers of the gospel, not being apostles nor successors of the apostles, are invested with no apostolic authority ; and, not being elders or bishops, they have no official place or power in any church (except when temporarily invited by some church) ; but each one, in the church with which he is in covenant, is only a member till the church shall call him to office either as a deacon

or as an elder ; and if he be called to office as an elder laboring in word and doctrine, then the communion of the churches will require that his induction into office be approved by a council in order to his being recognized as pastor by the neighbor churches.

4. A minister who is not a member of some Congregational church, is not in fact, and ought not to be counted, a minister in connection with the churches and ministry of the Congregational order, though he may be worthy of confidence and fellowship by virtue of his responsible connection with some other body of evangelical churches.

CHAPTER II.

Ordination to the Ministry at Large.

1. As it was in the church at Antioch that Barnabas and Saul received their special call to the missionary work among the Gentiles, so, by parity of reason, the formal designation of a brother to the work of a minister at large ought always to proceed from some church cognizant of his gifts and graces, and therefore competent to judge, in the first instance, whether he is called of

God; nor ordinarily should the call for a council to ordain him proceed from any other church than that in which he is, or in which he is to be a member.

2. As Barnabas and Saul, when sent from the church at Antioch on a mission to the Gentiles, were separated to their work by prayer and laying-on of hands; so it is fit, that, after reasonable trial, those who are called to minister in the word of God without holding the office of elders or bishops in any church be solemnly commended to the grace of God, and, by the laying-on of hands and prayer, be separated to the work whereunto he hath called them. No church ought to ordain any without the approval of neighbor churches assembled in a council. Yet it should be remembered that the ordination is the act of the church, and that the duty of such council is not to exercise jurisdiction or authority over the church, but simply to advise and assist, and to express the fellowship of other churches in the transaction.

3. Especially should men who enter upon the ministry that they may be sent on a foreign, or other distant mission, be solemnly separated to that work by the advice and assistance of councils duly

convened. Thus receiving from churches at home the right hands of fellowship, they may go forth, under Christ's commission, to preach his gospel, to gather churches, and to set them in order until such time as those churches shall have become sufficiently instructed and confirmed for self-support and complete self-government.

CHAPTER III.

Associations of Ministers.

1. THE experience of our churches, from the beginning, has proved that the frequent consultation of ministers with each other, so that the watchmen may see eye to eye, is of great importance to their efficiency in their work; and the formal association of pastors, not excluding other ministers, for mutual counsel and helpfulness, is an arrangement which has been greatly blessed of God for the welfare of the churches and the advancement of religion.

2. An Association of ministers has no jurisdiction or authority over the churches. It may give advice to its own members, or to any other person

asking its advice, on questions of church order or questions of doctrine ; but it can neither inflict nor remove any church censure. It forms its own rules concerning the qualifications and conditions of membership, and in accordance with those rules it can admit members and exclude them ; but it can ordain no man to the ministry, nor can it depose any man from the ministry. If one of its members, whether a pastor, or a minister without pastoral charge, is guilty of an offence for which he should be deposed from the ministry, it may not only exclude him from its fellowship, but may bring the matter to the notice of the church to which he is responsible. Or if any minister or professed minister of scandalous or heretical character is presuming to officiate in the churches of the vicinity, the Association may take measures to bring the matter to the notice of the proper ecclesiastical authority, or, if necessary to the protection of the churches and the vindication of the ministry, may give public notice that he is not in their fellowship.

3. By the common consent and ancient usage of the churches in New England, the recognized Associations of pastors and other ministers are intrusted with the duty of examining those who are

to preach as candidates for the ministry, and of commending them to the churches by letters of approbation, so that untaught or otherwise unfit persons may not intrude themselves into the work of preaching. In some other parts of the United States, the Conferences or associations of churches have assumed that duty, Associations of pastors and other ministers having been not yet instituted.*

CHAPTER IV.

Candidates for the Ministry; their Education and the Trial of their Gifts.

1. INASMUCH as the work of ministering in the word of God, to the edification of the churches, and to the advancement of religion, requires not only natural gifts of intelligence and discretion and of utterance, but also a personal experience of the gospel as the power of God unto salvation, a hearty love to Christ and to the souls of men, and a comprehensive knowledge of the Holy Scriptures, and of the system of truth which they reveal, our fathers, at the beginning, made great endeavors and sacri-

* Compare Heads of Agr. ch. iv. § 1; ch. vi.

fices to establish colleges consecrated to Christ and the church, that a faithful and competently learned ministry might be provided for their posterity, and for the country which they were redeeming from the wilderness. Colleges under Christian influence and control, and founded primarily for the education of men whom the churches may call to the ministry, are among the foremost of the voluntary institutions which accompany the prosperity of churches walking in the faith and order of the gospel ; and the work of presiding and teaching in such institutions is a work in which consecrated ministers of the gospel may make full proof of their ministry, and may obtain a place among those who have turned many to righteousness.

2. In later times, the progress of society and the increase and wide diffusion of knowledge having changed, in some degree, the course of education in the colleges, so that other and special studies are now necessary to a full preparation for the ministry, theological seminaries have been founded, that those who offer themselves to the service of Christ in the preaching and defence of His gospel, and who have been disciplined by liberal studies, and enriched with general knowledge, may be

instructed in all kinds of sacred learning, and, under the guidance of teachers who are also able and faithful preachers of the word, and experienced in the care of souls, may, by God's blessing on their endeavors, prepare themselves for the largest usefulness in the churches that may call them to office, and in the work of preaching the gospel to every creature.

3. The credentials which a young man may receive from a college, or a theological seminary, are not sufficient for his introduction to the churches as a preacher. Still less may his own desire to preach, or the desire of his friends and the commendation he receives from them, authorize him to offer himself as a candidate for the ministry, or make it safe for congregations to employ him for the trial of his gifts. Even at the beginning, when the churches were few and not far distant from each other, it was soon found needful to institute some well-considered arrangement for the examination of candidates and their orderly introduction to the churches. And inasmuch as it devolves on the pastors and teachers of churches to feed the several flocks of which the Holy Ghost hath made them overseers, and to take heed whom they severally

introduce to preach the word, it was agreed that neighboring pastors should jointly exercise their right of examination and inquiry before recognizing or commending a candidate as qualified to preach in public. It is, therefore, a long-established usage in the communion of our churches, that no man is to offer himself as a candidate for the ministry, or is to be received as such, without having been examined and approved by some recognized Association of pastors.*

4. In the examination of a candidate, the Association, having received evidence of his standing as a member in full communion of some evangelical church, with other testimonials to his blamelessness in life and his attainments in knowledge, inquires of him concerning his experience of the power of godliness, the reasons of his desire and choice to preach the gospel, the studies he has pursued, his knowledge especially of the system of doctrine contained in the Scriptures, and his readiness in the exposition and application of the word of God ; and, having obtained satisfactory evidence of his fitness to preach in the churches for the trial of his gifts, the pastors and other ministers in that Asso-

* Compare Heads of Agr. ch. ii, § 7.

ciation assembled, certify their approbation in a written testimonial.

5. The person thus accredited is not yet recognized as a minister of the gospel, but is only a candidate for the ministry, temporarily commended to the churches that they may make trial of his fitness for that sacred work ; and, till he shall be duly ordained to the ministry, the testimonial given to him may be withdrawn whenever that Association, for any good reason, is no longer willing to be responsible for him.

As many as walk according to this rule, peace be on them, and mercy, and upon the Israel of God !

APPENDIX.

DECLARATION OF FAITH

*Adopted by the National Council at Plymouth, Mass.,
June 22, 1865.*

STANDING by the rock where the Pilgrims set foot upon these shores, upon the spot where they worshipped God, and among the graves of the early generations, we, Elders and Messengers of the Congregational churches of the United States in National Council assembled, — like them acknowledging no rule of faith but the word of God, — do now declare our adherence to the faith and order of the apostolic and primitive churches held by our fathers, and substantially as embodied in the confessions and platforms which our Synods of 1648 and 1680 set forth or reaffirmed. We declare that the experience of the nearly two and a half centuries which have elapsed since the memorable day when our sires founded here a Christian Commonwealth, with all the development of new forms of error since their times, has only deepened our confidence in the faith and polity of these fathers. We bless God for the inheritance of these doctrines. We invoke the help of the Divine Redeemer, that through the presence of the promised Comforter, He will enable us to transmit them in purity to our children.

In the times that are before us as a nation, times at once of duty and of danger, we rest all our hope in the gospel of the Son of God. It was the grand peculiarity of our Puritan Fathers, that they held this gospel, not merely as the ground of their personal salvation, but as declaring the worth of man by the incarnation and sacrifice of the Son of God; and therefore applied its principles to elevate society, to regulate education, to civilize humanity, to purify law, to reform the Church and the State, and to assert and defend liberty; in short, to mould and redeem, by its all-transforming energy, everything that belongs to man in his individual and social relations.

It was the faith of our fathers that gave us this free land in which we dwell. It is by this faith only that we can transmit to our children a free and happy, because a Christian, commonwealth.

We hold it to be a distinctive excellence of our Congregational system, that it exalts that which is more, above that which is less, important, and, by the simplicity of its organization, facilitates, in communities where the population is limited, the union of all true believers in one Christian church; and that the division of such communities into several weak and jealous societies, holding the same common faith, is a sin against the unity of the body of Christ, and at once the shame and scandal of Christendom.

We rejoice that, through the influence of our free system of apostolic order, we can hold fellowship with all who acknowledge Christ, and act efficiently in the work of restoring unity to the divided Church, and of bringing back harmony and peace among all "who love our Lord Jesus Christ in sincerity."

Thus recognizing the unity of the Church of Christ in all the world, and knowing that we are but one branch of Christ's people, — while adhering to our peculiar faith and order, we extend to all believers the hand of Christian fellowship upon the basis of those great fundamental truths in which all Christians should agree. With them we confess our faith in God, the Father, the Son, and the Holy Ghost, the only living and true God; in Jesus Christ, the incarnate Word, who is exalted to be our Redeemer and King ; and in the Holy Comforter, who is present in the Church to regenerate and sanctify the soul.

With the whole Church, we confess the common sinfulness and ruin of our race, and acknowledge that it is only through the work accomplished by the life and expiatory death of Christ that believers in him are justified before God, receive the remission of sins, and through the presence and grace of the Holy Comforter are delivered from the power of sin, and perfected in holiness.

We believe also in the organized and visible Church, in the ministry of the Word, in the sacraments of Baptism and the Lord's Supper, in the resurrection of the body, and in the final judgment, the issues of which are eternal life and everlasting punishment.

We receive these truths on the testimony of God, given through prophets and apostles, and in the life, the miracles, the death, the resurrection, of his Son, our Divine Redeemer — a testimony preserved for the Church in the Scriptures of the Old and New Testaments, which were composed by holy men as they were moved by the Holy Ghost.

Affirming now our belief that those who thus hold

"one faith, one Lord, one baptism," together constitute the one catholic Church, the several households
of which, though called by different names, are the
one body of Christ, and that these members of his
body are sacredly bound to keep "the unity of the
spirit in the bond of peace," we declare that we will
co-operate with all who hold these truths. With them
we will carry the gospel into every part of this land,
and with them we will go into all the world, and
"preach the gospel to every creature." May He to
whom "all power is given in heaven and earth" fulfil
the promise which is all our hope: " Lo, I am with you
alway, even to the end of the world." Amen.

THE CONSTITUTION

OF THE

National Council, adopted at Oberlin, O., November 17, 1871.

THE Congregational churches of the United States, by elders and messengers assembled, do now associate themselves in National Council:

To express and foster their substantial unity in doctrine, polity, and work; and

To consult upon the common interests of all the churches, their duties in the work of evangelization, the united development of their resources, and their relations to all parts of the kingdom of Christ.

They agree in belief that the Holy Scriptures are the sufficient and only infallible rule of religious faith and practice; their interpretation thereof being in substantial accordance with the great doctrines of the Christian faith, commonly called Evangelical, held in our churches from the early times, and sufficiently set forth by former General Councils.

They agree in belief that the right of government resides in local churches, or congregations of believers, who are responsible directly to the Lord Jesus Christ, the One Head of the church universal and of all particular churches; but that all churches, being in communion one with another as parts of Christ's catholic church, have mutual duties subsisting in the obligations of fellowship.

The churches, therefore, while establishing this National. Council for the furtherance of the common interests and work of all the churches, do maintain the Scriptural and inalienable right of each church to self-government and administration ; 'and this National Council shall never exercise legislative or judicial authority, nor consent to act as a council of reference.

And for the convenience of orderly consultation, they establish the following Rules : —

I. *Sessions.* — The churches will meet in National Council every third year. They shall also be convened in special session whenever any five of the general State organizations shall so request.

II. *Representation.* — The churches shall be represented at each session, by delegates, either ministers or laymen, appointed in number and manner as follows : —

1. The churches, assembled in their local organizations, appoint one delegate for every ten churches in their respective organizations, and one for a fraction of ten greater than one half, it being understood that wherever the churches of any State are directly united in a general organization, they may, at their option, appoint the delegates in such a body, instead of in local organizations, but in the above ratio of churches so united.

2. In addition to the above, the churches united in State organization appoint by such body one delegate, and one for each ten thousand communicants in their fellowship, and one for a major fraction thereof : —

3. It being recommended that the number of

delegates be, in all cases, divided between ministers and laymen, as nearly equally as is practicable.

4. Such Congregational general societies for Christian work, and the faculties of such theological seminaries, as may be recognized by this Council, may be represented by one delegate each, such representatives having the right of discussion only.

III. *Officers.*— 1. At the beginning of every stated or special session, there shall be chosen by ballot, from those present as members, a moderator, and one or more assistant moderators, to preside over its deliberations.

2. At each triennial session, there shall be chosen by ballot a secretary, a registrar, and a treasurer, to serve from the close of such session to the close of the next triennial session.

3. ●The secretary shall receive communications for the Council, conduct correspondence, and collect such facts, and superintend such publications, as may from time to time be ordered.

4. The registrar shall make and preserve the records of the proceedings of the Council ; and for his aid, one or more assistants shall be chosen at each session, to serve during such session.

5. The treasurer shall do the work ordinarily belonging to such office.

6. At each triennial session, there shall be chosen a provisional committee, who shall make needful arrangements for the next triennial session, and for any session called during the interval.

7. Committees shall be appointed, and in such manner, as may from time to time be ordered.

8. Any member of a church in fellowship may be

chosen to the office of secretary, registrar, or treasurer ; and such officers as are not delegates shall have
the privileges of members, except that of voting.

IV. *By-Laws.* — The Council may make and alter
By-laws at any triennial session.

V. *Amendments.* — This constitution shall not be
altered or amended except at a triennial session, and
by a two-thirds vote, notice thereof having been given
at a previous triennial session, or the proposed altera-
tion having been requested by some general State
organization of churches, and published with the noti-
fication of the session.

BY–LAWS.

I. In all its official acts and records, this body
shall be designated as THE NATIONAL COUNCIL OF
THE CONGREGATIONAL CHURCHES OF THE UNITED
STATES.

II. It shall be understood that the term for which
delegates to the Council are appointed expires with
each session, triennial or special, to which they are
chosen.

III. The term "Congregational," as applied to the
general benevolent Societies, in connection with representation in this body, is understood in the broad
sense of societies whose constituency and control are
substantially Congregational.

IV. The Provisional Committee shall consist of
seven persons by appointment, with the addition of
the Secretary, Registrar, and Treasurer, *ex-officiis.*
This committee shall specify the place, and the precise

time, at which sessions shall commence; shall choose a preacher of the opening sermon; may select topics regarding the Christian work of the churches, and persons to prepare and present papers thereon; shall do any work which shall have been referred to them by the Council; and shall make a full report of all their doings, — the consideration of which shall be first in order of business after organization.

V. The sessions shall ordinarily be held in the latter part of October, or the early part of November.

VI. The call for any session shall be signed by the chairman of the Provisional Committee and the Secretary of the Council, and it shall contain a list of topics proposed by the committee; and the Secretary shall seasonably furnish blank credentials, and other needful papers, to the scribes of the several local organizations of churches.

VII. Soon after the opening of a stated or special session, the following committees shall be appointed:

1. A committee on Credentials, who shall prepare a roll of members.

2. A committee on Nominations, to nominate all committees not otherwise provided for.

3. A Business Committee, to propose a docket for the use of the members. Except by special vote of the Council, no business shall be introduced which has not thus passed through the hands of this committee.

Committees shall be composed of three persons each, except otherwise ordered.

VIII. In the sessions of the National Council, half an hour shall every morning be given to devotional services, and the daily sessions shall be opened with prayer, and closed with prayer or singing. One evening at least shall be entirely set apart for a meeting of prayer and conference; and every evening shall ordinarily be given to meetings of a specifically religious, rather than business character. And the Council will join in the sacrament of the Lord's supper at some convenient season.

IX. An Auditor of Accounts shall be appointed at every session.

X. The Provisional Committee may fill any vacancies occurring in any committee or office in the intervals of sessions, — the person so appointed to serve until the next session.

XI. The Council approves of an annual compilation of the statistics of the churches, and of a list of such ministers as are reported by the several State organizations. And the Secretary is directed to present at each triennial session, comprehensive and comparative summaries for the three years preceding.

XII. The Council will welcome correspondence by interchange of delegates, with the general Congregational bodies of other lands, and with the general ecclesiastical organizations of other churches of Evangelical faith in our land. Delegates will be appointed by the Council in the years of its session, and by the Provisional Committee in the intervening years.